MIND ON FIRE

a collection of poems by Jett Giessuebel

MIND ON FIRE
Copyright © 2021 Jett Giessuebel
ISBN: 978-0-578-24865-3
Printing: Kindle Direct Publishing & IngramSparks
Formatting: Bruce Freehoff
Cover Design: Bruce Freehoff
Editors: Sophia Elaine Hanson & Cheyenne Raine
Author Photo: Sara Jayne Giessuebel
(@sarajaynephotographyllc on Instagram)

**Part one of the
REBORN FROM CHAOS
trilogy**

Trigger Warnings:

anxiety
depression
panic attacks
suicide
suicidal ideation
self harm
eating disorders
paranoia
schizophrenia
hallucinations
anger issues
violence
violent thoughts
fire
bugs
gunshots
scars
knives
negative self image
trichotillomania
dermatillomania
drowning
& possibly more

Please be warned! This is an EXTREMELY triggering poetry collection about sensitive topics, as listed above. Practice self-care before, during, and after reading.

If you do not feel you can handle reading this content, please put it down.

Your mental and emotional well being is more important than reading a book.

To

Captain America: The Winter Soldier

& Bucky Barnes specifically.

Thank you for helping me survive

my high school years

Dear Reader,

The following collection is comprised of pieces I wrote when I was in my late teenage years while I was having an extremely difficult time dealing with my mental illnesses. I still have some of the same issues, however I am a lot healthier, happier, and stable.

All of these poems hold relevance in at least one way or another, but the overall severity and brutality of the moments recorded will (hopefully) remain a time capsule for me to look back at as I get older. A time capsule to remind myself how strong I am and just how far I've come.

If I could talk to my younger self, I would tell her many things. Other than the fact that I actually published a book, I would tell her that she is stronger & braver than she thinks. I would tell him that things will eventually get better, a lot better, actually. I would tell him that hope and love and happiness exist in many things, if they look hard enough. I would tell them that she is loved and important and valued. I would tell my younger self that I love her and I would let him in on the fact that in five years from where they are (now in 2021) I'm okay.
I am truly and honestly okay.

For everyone struggling with the issues that I did, that I do, I would tell you the same thing: Life gets better. You will get better. And no matter what your brain may tell you, people would miss you.

I wrote this collection to express myself and my feelings. I wrote it to cope and to heal, even though my words and thoughts are/were dark. I didn't want to sugarcoat what I went through or what I felt, so I didn't. This was what it was like for me, this was how I was, but I am and have always been more than just my mental illnesses. And so are you.

Please take care of yourself while reading this collection and step away if needed, and however long is needed.

Sincerely,

Jett

"I can't control their fear, only my own."

- Wanda Maximoff
  Captain America: Civil War (2016)

Mind on Fire

The nightmares start to take form.
The shadows grow hands
and the hands reach out to grab me.
The voices in my head start to scream.
I cry myself to sleep each night.
I see things that other people don't see.
I hear things that other people don't hear.
I feel things that other people don't feel.
And I eventually found out why.

- March 28, 2014

In the war between you and your mind,
you are a prisoner.
A prisoner to your thoughts,
a prisoner of war.

The Chaos and the Calm

You look at what your mind has become, and you think your mind
is the chaos and life is the calm.

The calm is the streak of sunlight poking out from behind the
storm clouds, the waves that still in the sea, the cease fire of bullets
in a raging war.

Your mind is a wreck and you stay there waiting for the next attack.

The first time it happens you toss and turn,
rip at your hair,
tear at your skin,
cry your eyes out,
your mouth open in a silent scream for help
as you wait for the madness to end.

You don't tell anyone until months later,
but how were you supposed to know that those nights were just the
beginning?

That they were the calm and you hadn't even begun
to see the chaos.
The chaos is when you relapse after months of remission.
It'll hit you like a downpour,
and when it does,
you will finally understand
that this is the chaos and that was the calm.

Labyrinth

Overgrown weeds and dangerous flowers,
a patch of desert and cracks in the earth,

an ocean constantly in the state of a hurricane.

A little girl stands in the middle of the rain
and every time she tries to jump in the puddles
the thunder booms and the lightning strikes the trees behind her.

Wolves fighting over a carcass,

a tornado off in the distance,
coming closer and closer with each passing second.

It's a labyrinth, my mind.
Confusing and misleading.

A labyrinth of hopes and dreams, of fears and doubts,

depression and anxiety intertwined —

disaster.

Carry

My flaws are close to my heart,

and my flaws are in my fists.

I carry my thoughts in my eyes

and my regrets in my head.

I carry all of these things,

it's no wonder I can't carry myself.

Is this what recovery feels like? Am I supposed to have breakdown after breakdown? Am I supposed to be struggling so much? Shouldn't I be making even the slightest bit of progress? Instead of none.

- recovery?

Mind on Fire

I haven't been to therapy in over a week

and the tiny piece of sanity I hold onto is slipping out of my hand.

Deep breaths.

Inhale

Exhale

Inhale

Exhale

It doesn't work as great as it does in a therapy session,

nothing does really.

It seems I can only stay afloat,

calm and steady,

if I'm in a therapy session.

Nowhere else.

Mind on Fire

You're the killer and I'm the victim

- mental illness

My Creator

I wonder if I'll ever meet my creator. I'd ask them,

> "Why was I made like this?"

I wonder if I'll ever meet my creator. I'd ask them,

> "Why has my entire existence shifted to revolve around
> one giant mental health problem?"

I wonder if I'll ever meet my creator, but I guess
I already have, because I've met my mom and I've
met my dad.

And they can't give me the answers to my questions,

so, I guess meeting my creator didn't do a damn thing.

Mind on Fire

I want it all to stop: the pain, the suffering, the tears

I want it all to go away: my worries, my fears

I want it all to end: my life

Mind on Fire

When it first started happening
I thought I was seeing ghosts,
and I honestly don't know which one
I'd prefer.

- are they hallucinations or are they ghosts?

"What are you afraid of?" she asks.

"Myself," I answer.

"What frightens you?" she asks.

"Everything," I tell her.

"What terrifies you?" she asks.

"Being forgotten," I whisper.

It's hard fighting your mind. It knows all of your tactics and your strategies for defense. Your mind is a good soldier, too bad it's not on your side.

Your mind tricks you, deceives you, misguides you, and fools you

- you are your own double agent

Mind on Fire

I am not Atlas and I never will be.
Atlas can hold up the world
and I can't even hold myself up.

Impossible

Is it impossible for me to be loved?
It feels that way.

It feels like it's impossible to dream in a world full of
hate and cruelty.

I used to wish on the first star I saw in the night sky.
It feels impossible for them to come true now.

I want my life to mean something. *And Holy shit, that feels as
impossible as it can get.*

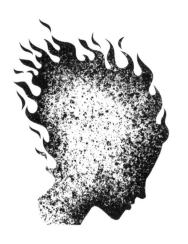

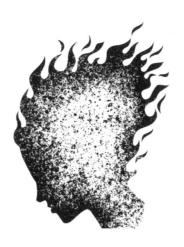

One of the things that keeps me going, if only a little, is the possibility of me being something. The possibility of it is what I try to grab onto. Because I know that if I knew for certain that I wouldn't become anything, I would kill myself.

- it's as simple and as horrifying as that

Let me be brave

Believing in something,
a cause or a dream,
is easier for me than believing in myself.
You should really believe in yourself first.

I believe in multiple possibilities,
in a wide range of experiences,
in different earths and different universes.

And I pray to every single one of them,
that if only one thing could go right in my world,
let me be brave.

Let me be kind.
Let me be confident.
Let me be strong.

But please, for the love of god, if nothing else, please,

let me be brave.

You were always one to tear yourself down just to
build someone else up.
Been that way since childhood, though that shouldn't surprise you.
Kids can be cruel and you grew insecure in the shadow of their
taunts, them tearing you down to build themselves up.

- the opposite but still a problem

Barely above water

For the past several years I've been trying to swim,
though I've never been good at swimming.
I've barely been holding my head above water
Even if the water is calm, even if it's still,
I'm barely above the water.
Then the waves come in and I'm sucked down again;
I'm drowning. I'm trying to hold on, my head is pounding,
and my throat is closing and my vision is going black.
I think I'm dead but then I find myself floating to the top.
I'm back to barely above water.

You remember the countless times you've screamed into the void, waiting for it to give you the answers you desperately wanted, needed.

- you still haven't gotten them

Mind on Fire

Some people die before they find
what they were searching for
and I hope to god

- I'm not one of those people

You are one in seven billion people in this world and to the
majority of them you don't matter

- a sad truth

You are one in a sea of billions and sometimes the
little fish gets eaten

- a sad truth, part two

Mind on Fire

Trust needs to be earned

- and I hand out mine like Halloween candy

Mind on Fire

I feel like I'm choking,

like my throat is closing,

and it hurts to breathe.

I kind of just want to finish the job

   - but I refuse to

Letting people go might be the right decision, but
that doesn't make the ache of their absence go away
any faster

- goodbyes will always hurt, at least to me

Believe in yourself.
Latch onto that belief,
hold it within your grasp,
and never let it go.

    - you'll need it

It is foolish to think you are the only who is hurting in the world
and it is naive to think love cures all.
It doesn't.

I'm the type of person who needs to have an actual wound to feel like I'm fighting. Without it I just feel fake, like an imposter, though I don't know a single person who would want what I have.

- the fight is in my head

On this scale, I cry
On this scale, I am at my lowest point

Here I crumble
Here I break
Here I die on the inside

On this scale, I bare my soul
On this scale, my heart is crushed

People leave, even when they said they'd stay. You can fall out of love. Someone who you thought you'd be with forever can mean nothing to you. Life isn't fair and there's nothing you can do about it. Nothing in life is guaranteed, not even happiness.

- hard to swallow

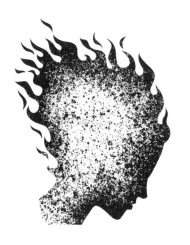

Mind on Fire

I'm stuck with myself forever and I may always feel this way.
I might spend my whole life trying to get better, but never succeed.

- hard to swallow, part two

For Someone Who

For someone who claims to be okay,
I sure breakdown a lot.

For someone who claims to be happy,
I sure am depressed a lot.

For someone who insists that they aren't suicidal,
I sure want to kill myself a lot.

For someone who says they want to live,
I sure think about my death a lot.

For someone who tells the doctors they aren't paranoid,
I sure get scared of everything around me a lot.

You owe it to yourself
to do everything you can
to keep dreaming

Mind on Fire

A lot can happen in a day, but you can't expect
everything to happen

- it's unrealistic

I used to be scared to get angry,
now I'm scared to get sad

  - oh, how times have changed

Mind on Fire

You don't have to be strong like them,
you just have to be strong like you

- superheroes

Mind on Fire

I raise my glass in a silent salute to those who are trying

- they are so much better than me

I can't stand to look at myself in the mirror, to look and see what
I've become

   - I'll hate what I see

Mind on Fire

She laces her own fingers together in a promise to herself,
to never get lost for too long

- a wanderer

Your interests don't have to be your talents
and your talents don't have to be your interests.

- don't let them lie to you

You cannot bare the weight of the world on your small shoulders.
You can only take so much before you break
and you cannot blame yourself for breaking
under the pressure of the universe

- you are only human

Mind on Fire

All you can really do in life is try your best
and sometimes your best isn't enough

- that might take me forever to really process

I tend to throw in my towel before anything bad has
a chance to happen

- that is not a good way to live

Mind on Fire

The ground shakes when she walks,
I wish I had that kind of power

- she creates earthquakes

You are important,
no matter what anyone else says,
even if that person is yourself.
You are important
and you always have been
and you always will be.
You are important.

The Science Experiment and the Scientist

Part one:

I am a science experiment.
I am poked and jabbed.
I am tested upon.
The people who do this to me
are looking for the perfect combination,
the super soldier serum.
I am given different pills
and the effects are recorded
on sheets of paper.
Sometimes the results are
encouraging,
other times they are
chaotic.
I am not a scientist,
I am what they create.

Part two:

I am a scientist.
I test theories to gain knowledge
about the reactions that occur.
I record my data
and then test it again.
I research everything to try
and understand how things work,
how the world works.
I create
and I destroy.
I am not a science experiment,
I am the one who creates them.

My soft heart is turning cold, solid.
Ice.
Stone.
All the good parts of myself flaking away,
my love cracking under the pressure.
Changing
Changing
Changing
A snowstorm where sunshine used to be.

Unlike when a clock's battery runs out and it stops, time does not. It keeps ticking by without anyone realizing it, sometimes without them at all. Time leaves people in the past and I'm trying my best not to get lost in it.

If anyone asks about my ending,
tell them
that I could finally breathe again.

   - suicide note

To my friends and family:

In my death, you will be set free.

- suicide note, part two

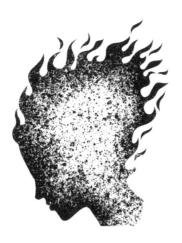

"I should just kill myself."

"No, fight to live."

"Fuck you, I'm tired of fighting."

"It won't be this way forever."

Everyone keeps leaving me.

I wish I was one of them.

It feels like I've been punched repeatedly in the gut.
Over and over again.

Like the wind has been knocked out of me.

Like freezing cold water has been thrown on me.

Like the ocean's waves are crashing into me from all sides, shoving me this way and that, until the only way to go is under.

- what losing you feels like

I saw the devastation coming.
I just never thought it would come in the form of this.

- you leaving

Can I be mad? Am I allowed to be angry?

I knew. I *knew*. She told me she had it.

I never thought I would get it.

Out of all of the problems I have, it wasn't one of them.
Until it was.

   - this eating problem, it runs in the family

Mind on Fire

I welcome the darkness
that looms over my head
because it's what I need

- pain grounds me

The line between fiction and reality is blurry and
I can't really trust my own mind.

My world around me is uncertain, nothing concrete in my head on
whether my surrounding are real, true. Or fake, only true to
my fractured mind.

My five senses combine and do nothing to help me
determine between

the fantasy my mind has conjured up and the ordinary
landscape that

surrounds everyone, even me.

The line between fiction and reality is hazy and I can't count on
myself to tell the difference.

- schizophrenia

Mind on Fire

After everything I've lost,
I can't afford to lose myself
more than I already have

- but I'm afraid I will anyway

"Everyone's mad here"

but no matter how many times I say it,
it still feels like just me

- I feel like the Mad Hatter and god do I hate Wonderland

Ode to 'Alice's Adventures in Wonderland' by Lewis Carroll

Mind on Fire

I can't wait ten or twenty years to see improvement.

I can't wait until I'm in my fifties to feel whole again.

I've never been a patient person

    - and that's just too long to wait

We'll go to war against ourselves.
It'll be hell,
but it can't be worse than now.

Wounds that won't heal,
exhausted but
ready to fight for our survival.

Focused on winning,
so we don't feel this way again.

- we'll go to war if it means peace

The Arsonist

The smoke relaxes her. The crackle of the flame is her
favorite kind of music.
She isn't fire, she's a spark, and that has to count for something.

She is everything you've been taught to avoid, yet here you are
getting caught in her reach.

She has goals, dreams. She wants to set the world on fire.

She wants to burn things down to start over, from scratch
or from flame.

She wants to make someone feel something, something passionate.

It's a desire. A subtle itch that gets harder and harder to ignore.

She's staring at an open flame and breathing in the smoke of
people's cigarettes.

She wants to destroy something the way her mind destroyed her.

She doesn't have a fire inside of herself, so she'll have to make one
on the outside.

Mind on Fire

Desperate to be loved
Guilty over the past
Depressed in the present
Anxious about the future

  - about myself

I do it when I'm anxious.
I do it when I'm bored.
I do it when I'm trying to concentrate.

It's a habit.
It's a disorder.
It's a problem.
I can't stop.

- picking

She embraces change,
the good and the bad.

    - she is not me

Mind on Fire

I am not afraid of what I am capable of.
I am afraid of what other people are capable of.

- uneasy

It's the coward's way out,
I know.
But I've never thought of myself as brave.

It's a selfish thing to do,
but then again,
I've never thought of myself as selfless.

  - suicide

You are a thorn in everyone's side, a blister on a foot.
You are not going anywhere.

- these are lies

Lying is easy. It's telling the truth that's hard.

Mind on Fire

I am angry about it,
but I am used to it.

I am used to it,
but I am not at peace with it.

- peace will never be an option,
  I don't know why I thought it would be

They may fade on the outside
but they will never fully heal on the inside

- scars

Are my demons happy?
Are they happy now that I can't remember a time without them?
I hope they are.
It would make one of us.

Mind on Fire

I don't know if I will ever be satisfied with my life

- but I promise I will try my hardest to be

Somewhere between the first diagnosis and the fifth, knowing how to act normal became lost in translation.

New Normal

Taking medication in the morning.
Taking medication at night.
Therapy sessions once a week.
Doctor's appointments once a month.
Daily mental breakdowns.
Crying at every mild inconvenience.
This is my new normal.

Mind on Fire

The storm is brewing,
you can see it in her eyes.
Tears are pouring down her face,
her voice is louder than thunder.

She's furious.
She'll hit you where it hurts.
She'll kiss you,
then hurt you.

When the stress builds
and the tension is high,
she'll lock her door,
fall to her knees,
and scream.

She'll push every emotion down
then throw punches to let it all out.
Knuckles black and blue,
the storm is here.

- she's a hurricane

I would die for what I believe in.

- am I a martyr or just suicidal?

Sometimes before you can save the world,
you have to save yourself.

I say "sorry" a lot, but I don't really regret much

- sorry is still my most used word

Mind on Fire

When you are constantly suicidal, the future is a fool's dream

- and I'm the fool who can't stop thinking about it

Mind on Fire

I would gladly let other people suffer
if it meant that I wouldn't anymore.

- does that make me selfish?

She will do what it takes to survive,
no matter the consequences

    - and that is precisely the problem

Pain makes me feel alive.
I thought I wanted to die,
but I think I just wanted to hurt

- unhealthy coping mechanisms

They are incurable.

You can get help,
but nothing can heal you,
nothing can fix you.

They can calm
or go dormant,
but they are still there,
waiting to come alive again.

They will be there,
always and forever,
until death do you part.

- mental disorders

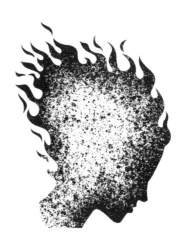

My stomach is in a constant state of ache,
too empty,
eat.
No.
Too full,
starve.
Okay.
I miss when this wasn't an issue.

Outsider looking in

I am there, but not there.
Silent,
just watching,
always just watching.

There is a certain disconnect,
between me and them,
a certain secret,
I don't know.

I am an outsider,
in their group of friends.

They lead,
and I follow,
they laugh and joke,
I sit and stare.
I am the third wheel,
fourth wheel,
fifth wheel.

I am an observer,
a lonely one.
I am there but not there,
I am an outsider looking in.

You appeared,
and my grip on reality
faltered.

- hallucinations

My mind is on fire,
and I can't get the flame to go out

   - unstable

If I had known how painful growing up was when I was younger,
I wouldn't have rushed into anything.

If I had known I would grow up to be a ticking time bomb,
I would have learned to deal with my emotions better.

- but I didn't

You want crazy?

I'll show you crazy.

Hating myself is a bloodsport.

Mind on Fire

I would rather feel nothing
than feel everything,
but my mind can't seem to get the memo.

The holes in the wall remind me of when I couldn't control myself,
but there is a monster inside of me that still wants out
and the holes in the wall seem like a good place to start.

- better the wall than someone else

Unhinged

She's unhinged,
She's been this way for years.
She doesn't know if she'll ever come to see
the light of day.
Doesn't know if she'll ever get better.
All she knows is the voices.
All she knows is agony.

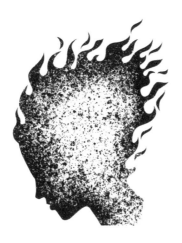

I don't know why I hold onto hope that things will get better,
that one day I will be good and pure,
because the writing has been on the wall
the whole time — I will continue
to live in hell
until the day I die.

I was put on death row when the doctor said "schizophrenia",
and I've been a dead man walking ever since

- but I will not be a statistic

I am made of metal and poison, strong enough to pick myself up
and strong enough to tear you down.

- mercury

She deals with her emotions in extremes
and she's not sure who will be stupid enough
to love her anyway

   - because it certainly won't be her

The thing about the universe
is that it doesn't owe you a damn thing.

But it feels like it could give you
fucking everything.

I hope for a life so extraordinary, that I never want to stop living it

- I know I'll be disappointed

Pimple

Rip

Blood

Scab

Rip

Blood

Scab

Rip

Blood

Scab

Rip

Blood

Scab

Rip

Scar

- picking, part two

They tell you that it's okay to cut toxic people out of your life and I agree. I've cut a few people out, but so many more cut me out. They leave as soon as they get the chance. Is it me? Have I been the one that needs to leave? Have I been the one that needs to change? What am I supposed to do if it's me that's toxic?

- how am I supposed to cut ties with myself?

My pride will be the death of me,
my pride will be the death of us all

- and I won't even notice until it's too late

Is it possible to be full of hate and still be a good person?

Can you be a good person and be selfish?

Is it possible to be a good person and not care about
other people's feelings?

Can you be a good person and want to hurt people?

   - please tell me I'm a good person

There was no goodbye,
no final hug,
no last "I love you."

Just unanswered texts
and the act of clicking
the 'unfriend' button.

- we're not friends anymore

My hatred for myself
bleeds into my hatred
for other people

    - and that is not fair to either of us

Tally Marks

There are one hundred and fourteen tally marks on my wall.
My parents ask what they're there for.
They've been there for years
but they still ask,
as if they see them for the first time each time they
come into my room.
I always lie and say I don't remember.
I say I don't remember why I marked them on my wall so dark
that they can't be erased.
I don't want to upset them by telling them the truth.
They're under the impression that I didn't start feeling
suicidal until I was sixteen,
but that's not true.
There are one hundred and fourteen tally marks on my wall.
There are one hundred and fourteen tally marks on my wall
for all of the times I wanted to die when I was fourteen.
One hundred and fourteen tally marks for each day
I wanted to die instead of living with the
voices and the visions.

Something metallic overcomes my taste buds.
Blood,
I taste blood.
I'm bleeding.
The taste gets stronger and stronger
until I am forced to swallow a mouth full of it.

I rush to the bathroom.
I'm scared to open my mouth
but I do so anyway.

I see teeth and tongue,
but no blood.
No cut or gashes,
and
no
blood.

-I was hallucinating again

I wanted my life to be like a John Hughes film, but what I got was
the exact opposite. I never went to a pep rally. I never skipped a
class to hang out with friends. I didn't have friends. I never went
to football games. I never got detention. I never had a high school
sweetheart. I didn't even have a two week sweetheart. I never went
to homecoming. I never went to prom. I never went to a party at
a classmate's house whose parents were out of town. I don't know
what the senior prank was. I don't know when senior ditch day was.
I was at home doing schoolwork more than I was at actual school.
I missed one hundred and fifty-three days of my senior year. I got
my diploma, but I can't really count what I experienced as high
school. I left that school with my almost nonexistent presence
affecting no one.

- those four years were a dark time

Mind on Fire

We went from six
to three
to two,
and god do I hope
we don't go back down to
one.

    - friend groups

Old scars mixed with new craters litter my back.
Shirts keep getting thrown away because the washing machine
can't take out the blood stains.
It doesn't seem to make a difference if my nails are long
or bitten short.
It doesn't seem to make a difference if the skin is clear
or blemished.
I still pick.
For small periods of time the urge goes away
and my skin starts to heal,
but the urge always comes back
and I always start to pick again.

- dermatillomania

Mental illness stole my teenage years and nothing I do can ever change that. Nothing I do can ever bring those years back. No matter how much I wish I could actually go to high school, so I don't feel like an idiot when I don't know something that I would've learned in sophomore year history class. No matter how much I beg for a second chance at my high school years, because while I don't actually want to go back, I know that no one there remembers me, and I wish that was different. No matter how much I scream, yelling at the sky for how shitty it is that I spent my teen years in group therapy sessions instead of at my desk in a classroom. You can't turn back time. You can't change the past. So nothing I ever do will change the fact that my mental illnesses stole what was supposed to be the best years of my life, and turned them into the worst.

- thief

I wasn't in love with you,
but I loved you,
and it still broke my heart
when you left

- friendships

I still took the emoji out of your contact name
on my phone.
I still unfollowed you on Instagram.
I still took down all of the pictures
I had of you on my wall.
I wasn't in love with you,
but I loved you,
and I still cried when you ended it.

- friendships, part two

I put on a fake smile and cheerfully said
"Good morning"
to fifteen people today.
Fifteen people that weren't actually there.

- hallucinations are annoying

Pain.
I am in pain.
Where is it coming from?
My stomach.
My stomach hurts.
Why does my stomach hurt?

My shirt to the left of my belly button
starts to feel damp
and clingy.
I touch it and my fingers come back
red and sticky.

I rip my shirt off
and there it is,
the source of my pain.
A hole in my body
that's pouring out blood.
A gun shot wound?
A gun shot wound!
I was shot!

Why didn't I hear the gun go off?
My stomach hurts.
I was shot.

(but I wasn't)

- hallucinations are terrifying

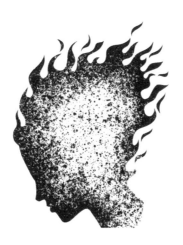

Dead at Eighteen

They ask,

"What are your plans for life?"

as if that's a simple question for me to answer.
And I guess for them, it is.

They don't know I didn't plan for the future.
They don't know I didn't plan on living past eighteen.

With the way my life was going,
I didn't think I'd make it that far,
so I didn't plan.

Now I'm scrambling to catch up to people
who have been planning for years.
I'm in last place in the competition of life,
when I didn't even want to compete in the first place.

"What are your plans for life?"

is not a simple question for someone who has been suicidal
since they were fourteen.
It's not a simple question for someone who thought they'd be
dead at eighteen.
Because the answer would have been,

"To die."

Maybe we knew each other in a past life.
Maybe we were best friends or sisters.
Maybe that's why we clicked instantly.
Maybe that's why I trusted you so quickly.
I'm not sure if I believe in destiny,
but I do believe I was meant to meet you.

Losing you would cripple me
and I never meant to get that attached.
You have worked your way into my soul
and you didn't even have to try.

You have helped me grow.
You have helped me become a better,
stronger person.
For that,
I thank you.

- L.B.

Hands that used to want to create
now want to destroy.

A voice that used to use words to help
now uses words to hurt.

I used to be full of love,
now I'm full of hate.

I've been surrounded by darkness for so long
that I've become it.

It has seeped into my pores
and worked its way into my heart.

I used to cry,
now I scream.

I used to be sweet,
now I'm sour.

  - how do I go back?

Every mistake,
every bad decision
weighs on me,
crushes me,
because I think it'll
drive you away.

Every argument
and every slammed door
fills me to the brim
with guilt,
because you don't deserve it.

You deserve better
than to be burdened
by my faults.

I drag you down
when all I've ever wanted to do
was make you proud.

- mom

Mind on Fire

I couldn't force you to stay,
even though I wanted to.
It does bring me a sick comfort though
that for once
it wasn't my mental illnesses
that drove you away.
It was yours.

I decide who hurts me.
I decide how I hurt myself.
I decide how I feel.
I decide how I heal.
I decide who I am.

- power

The teacher just finished taking attendance
when I smell it —
rotten eggs and acid.
My nose crinkles.
Why would I smell that?
The smell morphs into urine.
Did I pee my pants?
It goes on for a few minutes before it hits me

- I was hallucinating again, part two

I lose myself in movies
and songs.
I lose myself in books
and pictures.

And I can't exactly put into words
how nice it feels
to get lost in something
other than my mind.

Tattoos cover my forearms and wrists
in an attempt to stop me from cutting.
It helps,
but I'd have to cover every square inch
of my body in ink
to make sure I couldn't self harm.
Even then,
I'd still find a way
to hurt myself.

- tattoos only help so much

Static

When my thoughts get
out of control
I hear it —
the static.
It fills my ears
until it's all I can
hear.
It gets so loud that I
clamp my hands over my ears
to make it stop.
It never works.

Sometimes it goes away
after a couple of
minutes,
but sometimes it takes
hours
for the static to fully
leave my eardrums.

My body is filled with tension.
I have been trying to fight it,
fight the urge,
but it's too strong.
Where should I pull from now?
My scalp?
My eyebrows?
My eyelashes?
I'm in public so my privates
are out of the question.
How about all three?
I rip one
two
three eyelashes out
and the tension starts to ease.
I rip one
two
three
four
five
six eyebrow hairs out,
so I only have 3/4 of an eyebrow left.
It's not enough.
I rip one
two
three
four
five
six
seven
eight
nine
ten clumps of hair out of my head,
so I have to brush it a certain way
to hide a small bald spot.
I let the strands fall to the floor
and I walk away.
The tension has left my body,
but it will come back,
and then I'll pull again
and again
and again.

   - trichotillomania

Fire and Gasoline

Bad news will always come.
Bad things will always happen.
It's important to know what's going on
in the world,
but god help me,
when I'm informed
it amplifies everything.
It makes everything worse.
My mind gets more destructive,
more out of control,
more dangerous.
My mind is already bad enough on its own,
but adding outside hate and violence
is like dousing an already burning hot fire
in gasoline.

It torches everything in its path,
leaving behind only smoke
and ash.

My mental illnesses are fire.
Life is gasoline.
And I am a casualty of their cruelty.

All that makes me different is stolen from someone else.

Personalities stitched together, woven like a cloth from

fictional characters I adore and the people I surround myself with.

A mix and match pair of a heart and a soul,

with a brain too fucked up to repair.

I've reached the end of the line.

I can barely function.

I have no chances for survival.

I am

   - dead in the water

I'm a mess

Schizophrenia doesn't know love.
It doesn't know trust.
It knows chaos,
panic,
nightmares,
screams,
anarchy.

I'm a mess.

I'm one,
two threads away from being a
wardrobe malfunction.
I'm toxic waste dumped on a
playground.
I'm a glass of red wine
spilled onto a brand new
white carpet.

I'm a mess,
and people don't like messes.
Because when you try to clean it up,
it almost always gets on you,
and people don't like to get dirty.

I, it seems,
was always meant to live
a half life.

My mom doesn't like me watching scary movies.

I snap at her,

 "I'm an adult, mom. They're not even that scary."

She smiles sadly,

 "Sweetie, I don't want them to make your hallucinations worse."

I tell her,

 "They won't."

But they will and I know it, but I'm tired
of not being able to do certain things
because of my schizophrenia.
Even if it's something as little
as watching a scary movie.
Especially when it's something
as little as watching a scary movie.

 - schizophrenia takes and takes and takes

Not everyone is good hearted.
Not everyone is soft smiles and kind eyes.

Not everyone is caring.
Not everyone has good intentions.

Some people are bark and bite.
Some people use words
sharp as knives
to cut you down.

Some people will hurt others
to make themselves feel better.
Some people are cruel.

   - is it possible to be both?

The hanging tree
in my dreams
as a child
looms in my past
like a reaper

- things unchecked

A note to others:
I'm sorry. I never wanted you to bleed.

A note to myself:
To bleed is all I wanted you to do.

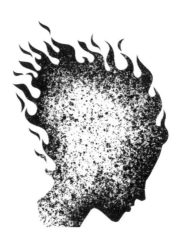

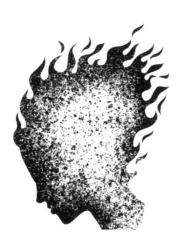

I'm losing my mind trying to get it back.

Mind on Fire

My fears surround me
like molten lava,
and while I have always
been one to flirt with fire,
I've never been one for
being burned alive.

It gets a little easier again.

I don't think I'll ever be ready for change,
even the good kind.

Things I lost to my mind on fire:

- friendships
- trust in people
- familial bonds
- affection
- happiness
- smiles
- school attendance
- my social life
- stability
- my love for life
- perception of reality
- peace & quiet
- love for nature & the outdoors
- adolescence
- my education
- compassion
- hope
- clear skin
- clumps of hair
- confidence
- passions
- TV shows or movies I would/could watch
- a will to live
- sanity
- my easy-going vibe
- belief of my own eyesight, hearing, and feeling receptors
- everything I hold dear, with or without knowing

Inspired by "Things we lost in the fire" by Bastille

I've always wanted to be a fighter,
a warrior.
Strong.

Maybe I should
fight to live
after all.

To die at a young age
is to be immortal,
forever frozen in time.

But is immortality worth it
if all I have to show for it
is my depression?

    - I can't risk losing my developing happiness
      because of my sick fantasies

The only person you have to make proud is yourself.

- everyone else is irrelevant

If I were to boil everything a hero is
down to their essentials,

I would find bravery despite fear
and a refusal to give up,
even if the odds are
stacked against them.

Many things go into making a hero
but those two things...

If I could just do those two things,
be those two things,

maybe I could be a hero, too.

NO. NO. NO.

My mental illnesses may have taken over my life,
but they don't get to take it from my hands.

So I choose life over death.

I choose to stay alive and live whatever life
I can still carve out for myself,
if for nothing else,
then for spite.

I am not a phoenix,
but watch me be reborn from these ashes.

Living is hard, but dealing with the permanency of death
isn't much easier.

I am made up of tears and hate.
I am one half tragedy,
one half rage.

Sometimes when you heal & cope,
it's not done properly.

- healing doesn't mean healthy

I am not indestructible. No, not even close. But I know I am strong and when it comes to my own mind, I will survive. I always have and I always will.

Mind on Fire

My world crumbled into ruins
in the amount of time it takes
to say a thirteen letter word.

It took years for my world
to rebuild, to be even a fraction
of what it used to be.

- and it was still rebuilt crooked

My demons live in the
flames of my mind,
but when the heat
died out and the
frost came in,
they just
evolved.

Mind on Fire

The eyes are windows to the soul
and when I looked into hers
all I saw was ice.

To be continued...

Acknowledgements:

To my mom: Thank you for being my rock, my first supporter, my biggest supporter, my confidant, my best friend. I will never be able to repay you for all you've done for me, nor will I ever be able to truly tell you just how much you mean to me. You hold me up everyday and I would have nothing without you. I love you.

To Laura: Thank you for being in my life and putting up with me for the past six years. I very much believe you are one of my many platonic soulmates and that you're a part of my soul I will never let go of. I love you.

To my dad: Thank you for supporting my dreams and always listening to me when I say the same thing at least five times a day. Thank you for having my back, but also wanting to push me to be better. I love you.

To my brothers Justin & Cody: I love the two of you so much and I want to say thank you for all the support you've given me with this book and the care you've had with all of my struggles. Thank you for all of the encouragement but also all of the teasing (not so teasing) insults. Thank you for trying and thank you for not treating me too differently.

To my editor, Sophia: Thank you for reading my work and helping make it stronger.

To my second editor, Cheyenne: Thank you for bettering my grammar and reviewing the reader experience with your edits.

To Katie: Thank you so much for reading this collection and giving me your creative input, thank you for getting excited over things I message you or put on social media.

To McKayla: Thank you for being an inspiration to me & thank you so much for dealing with and answering all of the questions I have about self publishing. I don't know what I'd do without your help.

To my Uncle Bruce: Thank you for making my dream cover come to life. You did such an excellent job. I'm so grateful.

And to the reader: Thank you for taking the time and chance to read my poems. I appreciate the support and am forever grateful. I wrote this while I was struggling with my mental health but I'm still here today to write the rest of my story. I hope that you'll continue with me.

Always & Forever,

Jett

Resources:

National Suicide Prevention Lifeline: 1-800-273-8255

Substance Abuse and Mental Health Services Administration (SAMHSA) National Helpline: 1-800-662-HELP (4357)

National Alliance on Mental Illness (NAMI): 1-800-950-6264

Teen Line: 1-310-855-HOPE (4673)

or

1-800-TLC-TEEN (1-800-852-8336)

Boys Town National Hotline: 1-800-448-3000

yourlifeyourvoice.org

Crisis Text Line: text "connect" to 741741

References:

Captain America: Civil War.
Directed by Anthony Russo and Joe Russo.
Screenplay by Christopher Markus and Stephen McFeely.
Performances by Chris Evans, Robert Downey Jr.,
Scarlett Johansson, Elizabeth Olsen, Sebastian Stan, Paul Rudd,
Anthony Mackie, Paul Bettany, Jeremy Renner,
Chadwick Boseman, Don Cheadle, Tom Holland,
Emily VanCamp, and Daniel Brühl

Marvel Studios, 2016

About the author:

Jett grew up an avid reader with a passion for creating her own stories. She reads slowly, their to be read list growing daily. In love with far too many fictional characters, writing and reading modern poetry, Jett loves all forms of art.

Jett lives in New Jersey with his family. When they are not writing, he can be found creating collages of the characters she obsesses over, taking dozens of pictures at a time, rewatching their favorite movies or shows, or getting a new tattoo.

Please consider leaving a review on Amazon and/or Goodreads to support Jett's work.

You may find her at:
Instagram - @jettgiesswrites
Tik Tok - @buckybarnesstan
Twitter - @jettgiess
Facebook - @jettgiesswrites

CPSIA information can be obtained
at www.ICGtesting.com
Printed in the USA
BVHW040835040821
613614BV00016B/428